MW00563843

Trombone

Christmas Instrumental Solos

Popular Christmas Songs

Contents

Alfred Publishing Co., Inc.
16320 Roscoe Blvd., Suite 100
P.O. Box 10003
Van Nuys, CA 91410-0003
alfred.com

Arranged by Bill Galliford, Ethan Neuburg and Tod Edmondson

ISBN-10: 0-7390-4872-4
ISBN-13: 978-0-7390-4872-6

BELIEVE
(From "THE POLAR EXPRESS")

Words and Music by
ALAN SILVESTRI and GLENN BALLARD

28343

HAVE YOURSELF
A MERRY LITTLE CHRISTMAS

Words and Music by
HUGH MARTIN and RALPH BLANE

Moderately slow and gently (♩ = 100)

JINGLE BELL ROCK

Swing (♩ = 132) (♪♪ = ♪³♪)

Words and Music by
JOE BEAL and JIM BOOTHE

*C♭ = B♮

28343

O CHRISTMAS TREE
(O Tannenbaum)

Traditional German

rit.

SLEIGH RIDE

By
LEROY ANDERSON

Moderately bright, with spirit (♩ = 100)

WE WISH YOU A MERRY CHRISTMAS

Traditional English

WINTER WONDERLAND

Words by
DICK SMITH

Music by
FELIX BERNARD

28343

YOU'RE A MEAN ONE, MR. GRINCH

Lyrics by
DR. SEUSS

Music by
ALBERT HAGUE

28343

DO THEY KNOW IT'S CHRISTMAS?
(Feed the World)

Words and Music by
BOB GELDOF and MIDGE URE

Do They Know It's Christmas? - 2 - 1
28343

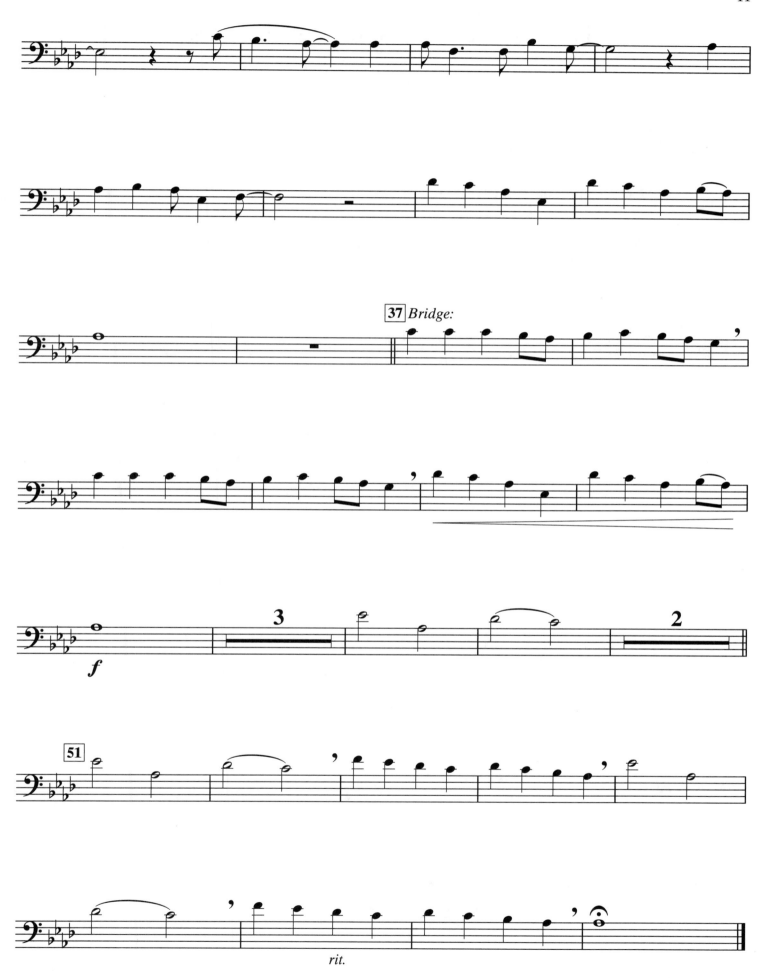

SANTA CLAUS IS COMIN' TO TOWN

Words by
HAVEN GILLESPIE

Music by
J. FRED COOTS

Up-tempo rockin' swing (♩ = 144)

Santa Claus Is Comin' to Town - 2 - 1
28343

GROWN-UP CHRISTMAS LIST

Words and Music by
DAVID FOSTER and
LINDA THOMPSON JENNER

Moderately slow (♩ = 72)

Grown-Up Christmas List - 2 - 1
28343

FELIZ NAVIDAD

Words and Music by
JOSÉ FELICIANO

PARTS OF A TROMBONE AND POSITION CHART

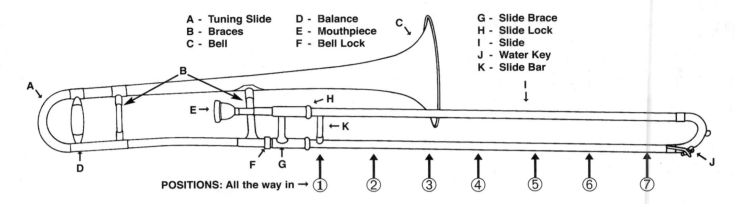

A - Tuning Slide   D - Balance   G - Slide Brace
B - Braces   E - Mouthpiece   H - Slide Lock
C - Bell   F - Bell Lock   I - Slide
                                                     J - Water Key
                                                   K - Slide Bar

POSITIONS: All the way in → ① ② ③ ④ ⑤ ⑥ ⑦

How To Read The Chart

The number of the position for each note is given in the chart below. See the picture above for the location of the slide bar for each position. When two enharmonic tones are given on the chart (F# and G♭ as an example), they sound the same and are played with the same position. Alternate positions are shown underneath for trombones with a trigger (T=thumb trigger).

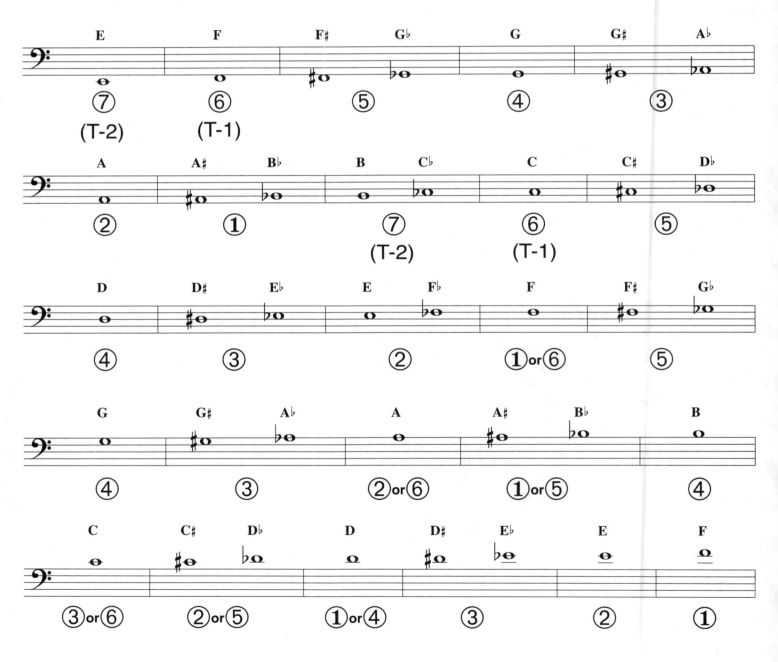